NEW BELIEVER'S SERIES

WATCHMAN NEE

SEEKING GOD'S WILL

17

Living Stream Ministry
Anaheim, CA • www.lsm.org

First Edition, November 1997.

ISBN 978-1-57593-973-5

Published by

Living Stream Ministry
2431 W. La Palma Ave., Anaheim, CA 92801 U.S.A.
P. O. Box 2121, Anaheim, CA 92814 U.S.A.

Printed in India

13 14 15 16 17 18 / 11 10 9 8 7 6 5

SEEKING GOD'S WILL

Scripture Reading: John 7:17; Matt. 10:29-31; 18:15-20; Rom. 8:14; Psa. 119:105; 1 John 2:27

I. THE NEED TO OBEY GOD'S WILL

Before we were saved, we did everything according to our own will. At that time we served ourselves and did everything to please ourselves. We would do anything as long as it pleased us or made us happy. However, now we have believed in the Lord and have accepted Christ Jesus as our Savior. We have acknowledged Him as our Master, the One whom we serve. We have acknowledged that He has redeemed us. We belong to Him and are of Him, and we are here to serve Him. For this reason, we need a fundamental change. We no longer should walk according to our preference; we must walk according to God's will. After we believe in the Lord, the focus of our living changes. The focus is no longer ourselves, but the Lord. The first thing we should do after we are saved is ask, "What shall I do, Lord?" Paul asked this question in Acts 22:10, and we should ask the same question. Whenever we come across a situation, we should say, "Lord, not as I will, but as You will." In making decisions or in choosing our paths, we should always say to the Lord, "Not as I will, but as You will."

The life we possess has one basic demand—to walk according to God's will. The more we obey God's will, the happier we become within. The more we deny our own will, the straighter our pathway will be before God. If we walk according to our own will as we once did, we will not feel happy. Instead, we will suffer. After we are saved, the more we walk according to our own will, the more suffering and the less joy we will have. But the more we walk according to the new life and the more we obey God's will, the more peace and joy we will have. This is a wonderful change. We should not think that we will be happy if we walk according to our own will. After becoming Christians, we will find our path filled with peace and joy if we do not walk according to our own will but learn to submit to and obey God's will. Christian joy has to do with obeying God's will, not with walking according to our own will.

Once we become Christians, we have to learn to accept God's will and be governed by it. If a person can submit humbly to God's will, he will spare himself many needless detours. Many fail and stop growing in life because they walk according to their own will. The result of walking according to our own will is nothing but sorrow and poverty. In the end we still have to walk according to God's will. God always subdues us through things, circumstances, and the environment. If we have not been chosen by God, He will let us walk as we wish. But since we have been chosen by God, He will lead us to the way of obedience according to His way. Disobedience will only cost us unnecessary detours. In the end we will still have to obey.

II. HOW TO KNOW GOD'S WILL

Our question now is how do we know God's will. We often think that mortals like us could never understand God's will. However, we should have the assurance that not only do we want to obey God's will, but God Himself also wants us to obey His will. Not only do we seek to know His will, but God Himself also wants us to know His will. If God wants us to obey His will, He must first enable us to know His will. Therefore, it is God's business to reveal His will to us. None of God's children need to worry and say, "Since I cannot know God's will, how can I obey it?" This concern is unnecessary because God always has a way to show us His will (Heb. 13:21). We have to believe that God will always show us His will through the proper means. It is God's responsibility to tell us His will. If we are submissive in our attitude and intention, we will surely know His will. All of us must learn to believe that God is eager to reveal His will to man.

What are the ways to know God's will? A Christian must pay attention to three things in order to know God's will. If these three things are in agreement with one another, we can be quite sure that it is God's will. These three things are: (1) arrangements in the environment, (2) the leading of the Holy Spirit, and (3) the teachings of the Scripture. These three things are not mentioned according to the order of their importance. They do not necessarily have to be in sequential order. We are simply stating that these three things help us know God's will. When the testimonies of these three things are in agreement with one another, we can be assured that we know God's will. If one of these three things is not in agreement with the other two, we still need to wait. We must wait until all three agree with one another before we go ahead.

A. Arrangements in the Environment

Luke 12:6 says, "Are not five sparrows sold for two assaria?" Matthew 10:29 says, "Are not two sparrows sold for an assarion?" If one assarion could buy two sparrows, then by right two assaria should only buy four sparrows. But the Lord said two assaria could buy five sparrows. One assarion buys two, and two assaria buy four plus an additional one. This shows us the cheapness of a sparrow. However, even a cheap thing such as a sparrow is not allowed to fall to the earth if God forbids it. Although the fifth sparrow is an extra one that is given for free, no sparrow is forgotten by God. If our God does not allow it, no sparrow can fall to the earth. This clearly shows us that everything happens under God's permission. If our heavenly Father forbids it, even a sparrow will not fall to the earth.

It is difficult to number a person's hairs. However, the Lord said, "Even the hairs of your head are all numbered" (Matt. 10:30). No one knows how many hairs he has, and no one can count his own hairs, but God has counted and numbered our hairs. Our God is so fine and so exact!

If God takes care of a seemingly worthless creature such as a sparrow, how much more will He take care of His children! If God takes care of something as minute as a hair, how much more will He take care of other things! Once we believe in the Lord, we need to learn to know His will through the environment. Nothing that happens to us is a coincidence.

Everything is measured by the Lord. Our career, spouse, parents, children, relatives, friends, and everything have been ordained by God. Behind everything that happens to us each day is God's sovereign arrangement. Therefore, we have to learn to read God's will in the environment. A new believer may not be that experienced in the leading of the Spirit, and he may not know that much of the teaching of the Scripture. But at least he can see God's hand in the environment. This is a believer's most basic lesson.

Psalm 32:9 says, "Do not be like a horse or like a mule, without understanding; / Whose trappings consist of bit and bridle to constrain them, / Else they do not come near you." Many times we are just like a horse or a mule, without understanding, and must be harnessed with outward bit and bridle by God before we can avoid mistakes. Have you ever seen a duck farmer? He has a long stick in his hand. When the ducks wander to the left or to the right, he herds them back with his stick. The ducks have no choice but to take the right path. In the same way, we can commit ourselves to the Lord and tell Him, "Lord, I am truly like a horse or a mule that has no understanding. But I do not want to make mistakes. I want to know Your will. Please harness me with Your bit and pull me with Your bridle. Once You let go of me, I will take the wrong way. Please guard me with Your will and direct me into Your will. If I wander away, I want You to stop me. I do not know many things, but I know what pain feels like. When I reject Your will, please come in and stop me!" Brothers and sisters, we must never belittle God's arrangement in the environment. Even though we may have fallen into shame and may have become like a horse or a mule, we often can still count on God's mercy to bridle us in time. God uses the environment to stop us from making mistakes. He forces us to have no alternative but to follow Him.

B. The Leading of the Holy Spirit

God's hand is seen through the environment. But He is not happy to always guide us like senseless horses or mules. He wants to guide us from within. Romans 8:14 says, "For as many as are led by the Spirit of God, these are sons of God." We are

God's children and God's life is within us. God not only guides us through the environment but also speaks to us and guides us from within through His Spirit. The Spirit dwells within us, and God's will is revealed to us through our innermost being.

The book of Ezekiel tells us that God will "put a new spirit within you" (11:19). Again it says, "A new spirit will I put within you....I will put my Spirit within you" (36:26-27). We must distinguish between "a new spirit" and "my Spirit." "My Spirit" refers to the Spirit of God, whereas "a new spirit" refers to our spirit at the time of our regeneration. This new spirit is like a temple, a home where the Spirit of God dwells. If we did not have a new spirit within us, God would not have given us His Spirit, and the Holy Spirit could not have dwelt within us. Throughout the ages God has been trying to give man His Spirit. However, man's spirit was defiled, sin-ridden, dead, and fallen in the old creation. It was impossible for the Spirit of God to dwell in man even though this was His desire. Man has to receive a new spirit through regeneration before he can be in the position to receive God's Spirit and before God can dwell in him.

Once a new believer has a new spirit, the Spirit of God dwells in him. The Spirit of God spontaneously communicates to him His will; he spontaneously has an inner sense. Not only is he able to discern God's provision in the environment, but he also now possesses an inward knowledge and inward assurance. We should learn to trust not only in God's sovereignty in the environment but also in the leading of the Holy Spirit within. At the right time and when the need arises, the Spirit of God will enlighten us within. He will give us a sense and show us what is of God and what is not of God.

One brother loved to drink before he became a believer. Every winter, he would drink much wine. He even made his own wine. Later, both he and his wife were saved. He was not very literate and could not read the Bible very well. One day he prepared some food and wine and was going to drink as before. After thanking the Lord for the food, he asked his wife, "Can a Christian drink wine?" His wife said, "I do not know." He said, "Too bad no one is here to tell us." His wife said, "The wine and the food are ready. Let us go ahead today and ask others afterward." He gave thanks again but felt that something was not right. He thought that, as a Christian, he should find out whether Christians can take wine. He asked his wife to take out the Bible, but he did not know where to turn. He was stuck. Later, he met someone and told him about this incident. His friend asked whether or not he drank the wine that day. He answered, "In the end I did not drink it, because the *householder within* would not allow me. I did not drink the wine."

If a man has the desire to obey God's will, he will find out what this will is. Only those who are callous about their inner sense will remain in darkness. As long as one has the intention to obey God's will, the "householder within" will guide him. The householder that our brother spoke of is actually the Holy Spirit. When a person believes in the Lord, the Holy Spirit dwells within him. He guides the believer and becomes his Master. God reveals His will not only through the environment but also through the "householder within."

There are two kinds of leading of the Holy Spirit. The first is an inner urging, as in Acts 8:29 when "the Spirit said to Philip, Approach and join this chariot" and in Acts 10:19-20 when the Holy Spirit said to Peter, "Rise up, go down and go with them." These are inner urgings. The second kind of leading is an inner forbidding, as mentioned in Acts 16:6-7: "Having been forbidden by the Holy Spirit to speak the word in Asia. And when they had come to Mysia, they tried to go into Bithynia, yet the Spirit of Jesus did not allow them." This is the inner forbidding. The story of the "householder within" is a case of inner forbidding.

In order to know God's will, a new believer should be somewhat familiar with the inner sense. The Spirit of God dwells in the innermost part of man. Hence, the feeling of the Spirit is not something shallow or outward; it issues from the deepest part of man's being. It is a voice that is not quite a voice, a feeling that is not quite a feeling. The Spirit of God within shows us whether something is according to His will. Provided we have the divine life within, we will feel right when we act according to this life, and we will feel terrible and uneasy within if we disobey and deviate slightly from this life. A believer should live a life that yields to this life. We must not do things that will take away our inner peace. Whenever we sense any unrest, we should realize that the Holy Spirit within is displeased with what we are doing; He is grieved. If we do something that is contrary to the Lord, we will surely have no peace within. The more we go ahead with it, the less peace and joy we will have. If something is of the Lord, spontaneously we will have peace and joy.

However, do not overanalyze your inward feelings. If you keep analyzing whether or not something is right, you will be totally confused. Some people continue to ask what the feeling of the Holy Spirit is and what the feeling of the soul is. They are always analyzing whether something is right or wrong. This is very unhealthy; it is actually a spiritual sickness. It is very difficult to bring a self-analyzing person back to the proper path. I hope that you can avoid such a trap. Actually, a person analyzes only because he does not have enough light. If he has enough light, everything will be clear to him spontaneously, and he will not need to waste his energy on such analysis. If a person is sincere in trying to obey the Lord, it will be very easy for him to sense the inner leading.

C. The Teachings of the Scripture

God's will is not only revealed through the environment and made known through the indwelling Spirit; it is also revealed to us through the Bible.

God's will never changes. His will is revealed through the various experiences of men of the past, and all these things were recorded in the Bible. God's will is revealed in the form of principles and examples in the Bible. To know God's will, one must study the Bible carefully. The Bible is not a book of simple records, but a book rich in content. God's will is fully unveiled through the Scripture. One needs only to find what God has said in the past, and he will know what God's will is today. God's will never wavers. In Christ there is only one yes (2 Cor. 1:19). God's will for us never contradicts the teachings of the Bible. The Holy Spirit will never lead us to do something today that He has already condemned in the Bible.

God's word is a lamp to our feet and a light to our path

(Psa. 119:105). If we want to understand God's will and His leading for us, we must study the Bible carefully and seriously.

God speaks to us through the Bible in two ways: One is through the teaching of biblical principles, and the other is through the promises in the Bible. We need the Spirit's enlightenment to understand biblical principles, and we need the Spirit's leading to receive biblical promises. For example, the Spirit may speak to us through the Lord's commandment in Matthew 28:19-20 that all Christians should preach the gospel. This teaching is a biblical principle. However, whether or not it is God's will for you to go to a certain place to preach the gospel depends on the leading of the Spirit. You still have to pray much and ask God for a specific word. When the Holy Spirit puts a certain phrase or verse within you in a powerful, fresh, and living way, you have a promise from the Spirit. This is how you identify God's will.

Some believers use superstitious ways to seek God's will. They open the Bible before them and pray, "O God, please move my finger to the verse which reveals Your will." After they pray with their eyes closed, they open their Bible and point their finger to any passage. Then they open their eyes and take the verse before them as God's will. Some childish believers try to know God this way. Because they are desperate, God will sometimes accommodate their ignorance and show them the way. However, this is definitely not the proper way. It will not work with most people, and it will not work most of the time. It is dangerous, and there is a great possibility for mistakes with this way. Brothers and sisters, please remember that we have the divine life and that God's Spirit is dwelling in us. We should ask God to reveal His word to us through the Holy Spirit. We should study the Bible conscientiously and consistently and memorize the Scripture well. When needs arise, the Holy Spirit will use the passages we have read to speak to us and to guide us.

Let us now combine the three things spoken of above. There is no fixed order for these three things. Sometimes, the arrangement of the environment comes first, followed by the leading of the Spirit and the teachings of the Bible. Sometimes, the Spirit's leading and the teachings of the Bible come first, and afterward, the confirmation in the environment. The environment is related especially to God's timing. In seeking after God's will, Brother George Müller always asked three questions: (1) Is it God's work? (2) Am I the person to do this work? (3) Is this God's time for such a work to be done? The first and second questions can be resolved by the teaching of the Bible and the leading of the Spirit. The third question is settled by provisions in the environment.

If we want to be sure that our inward feeling is the leading of the Spirit, we should also ask two questions: (1) Does this leading match the teaching of the Bible? (2) Does the environment confirm this leading? If such a leading does not match the teaching of the Bible, it cannot be God's will. If the environment does not give any confirmation, we should wait. Our feeling may be wrong, or it may not be the Lord's timing.

In seeking God's will, we should cultivate a healthy fear of making mistakes. We should not be subjective. We can ask God to block the ways that are not according to His will.

Suppose someone has invited you to work, and you have the intention to do a certain thing, or someone has advised you to reconsider your future, etc. How can you know whether these things are according to God's will? First, you should look at the teaching of the Bible. You should find out what God has actually said about such matters in His Word. After this, you should check with your inner feeling. The Bible may teach this, but do you feel right within? If your inward feeling is different from the testimony of the Bible, it proves that your inward feeling is not reliable. You should continue to wait and seek the Lord. If your inward leading agrees with the testimony of the Bible, you should lift up your head and say, "O Lord, You have always revealed Your will through the environment. It is impossible for my inward feeling and the teaching of the Bible to both point to one direction, and yet have the environment point to a contrary direction. Lord! Please work in the environment and line it up with the Scripture's teaching and the Spirit's leading." You will see that God always reveals His will through the environment. Not one sparrow will fall to the earth if it is not God's will. If it is God's will, what you see outwardly will surely line up with what you see inwardly and what you see from the Bible. If your inward sense, the teaching of the Bible, and the environment are all clear, then God's will for you will also be clear.

III. THE CONFIRMATION OF THE CHURCH
AND OTHER FACTORS

God's will is revealed through His Word, man's spirit, and the environment. God's will is also revealed through the church. In seeking God's will concerning a certain matter, you should be clear about the Spirit's leading, the Scripture's teaching, and the environment's provision. As much as it is possible, you should also fellowship with those who know God in the church to see whether they will say amen to your guidance. This will give you additional confirmation concerning God's will. These ones know God's Word more, their flesh has been dealt with somewhat, and they are under the direction of the Spirit. Their spiritual condition allows God to speak His heart more freely through them. They will consider your condition in the church, and they will sense whether or not they can say amen to what you have seen. If they can say amen, you can be sure that what you have is God's will. If they cannot say amen to it, it is better for you to wait and seek more guidance. As individuals, we are limited. An individual's personal feeling, understanding of the Scripture, and knowledge of the environment may be wrong; they may not be that accurate. The church is much more reliable in this respect. If the other members of the church think that the "guidance" you have is not reliable, you should not insist on your opinion. Do not think that your "guidance" is always reliable. In such cases we should learn to be humble.

Matthew 18 speaks of the principle of the church. If a brother sins against another brother, the offended one should speak to the offending one while they are alone with each other. If the offending party does not want to listen, the offended party should take with him one or two more. By the mouth of two or three witnesses, every word may be established. If the offending party still refuses to listen, the matter should be told to the church. In the end the offending one has to hear the church. We have to accept the feeling of the church. The

Lord Jesus says, "Whatever you bind on the earth shall have been bound in heaven, and whatever you loose on the earth shall have been loosed in heaven" (v. 18). Because the church is God's habitation and the beacon of God's light, we need to believe that God's will is revealed in the church. We should humble ourselves and should be afraid of our own judgment. This is why we need to fellowship with the church and receive the supply of the Body.

The church has a heavy responsibility before God. It has to act as God's light. If the church is careless or if it does things loosely according to the flesh, it will be impossible to have such a thing as the confirmation of the church. The church can render an accurate and divine confirmation because it has become the mouthpiece of the Holy Spirit. The church must be spiritual, and it must allow the Spirit to preside over it before it can be used by the Spirit to be God's mouthpiece. The confirmation of the church does not mean a discussion among all the brothers and sisters in the church together. It means the speaking of a group of people who know God and who are being led by the Spirit. For this reason, the elders taking responsibility in the church, as well as those given to the Lord's work, must have a certain amount of knowledge of spiritual things. Their flesh must be dealt with to a certain extent. They must be watchful at all times and have unceasing fellowship with the Lord. They must be full of God's presence and must live under the direction of the Holy Spirit. Only then can there be accurate judgment, and only then will the Spirit give accurate confirmation through them.

Some people may quote Galatians 1:16-17, which says that when Paul received a revelation, he did not confer with flesh and blood, neither did he go up to Jerusalem to see those who were apostles before him. They think that it is sufficient for them to be clear by themselves and that there is no need to fellowship with the church. No doubt a person with a clear revelation like Paul can be truly confident of what he sees. But have you received the revelation the way Paul received his? Even Paul received the Lord's help and supply through other brothers. He saw the great light on the way to Damascus, fell to the ground, and heard what the Lord said to him alone: "Rise up and enter into the city, and *it will be told to you what you must do.*" He received the laying on of hands from an obscure brother named Ananias, and he also received the laying on of hands and the commissioning from co-workers in the church in Antioch (Acts 9:3-6, 12; 13:1-3). The words he spoke in Galatians 1 were to prove that the gospel announced by him was not according to man, but that he had "received it through a revelation by Jesus Christ" (vv. 11-12). There is no flavor of self-exaltation in such words. We should be humble and not intractable. We must not think highly of ourselves. The fact is that we are too far behind Paul to compare ourselves to him! Because we are the party involved, we are clouded by our own interests and subjectivity when we seek God's will. It is difficult for us to see things clearly. This is where the church comes in; it can supply us and render us much help. This is why we should seek confirmation from the church when we are in need.

However, we should avoid another extreme. Some Christians are too passive. They ask the church about everything, and they want others to make decisions for them. This is against the principle of the New Testament. We cannot treat a group of spiritual people in the church as if they were the prophets in the Old Testament, asking them for advice in everything. First John 2:27 says, "And as for you, the anointing which you have received from Him abides in you, and you have no need that anyone teach you; but as His anointing teaches you concerning all things..." This anointing is the indwelling Holy Spirit. We can never replace the teaching of the anointing with the confirmation of the church. The confirmation of the church should not be regarded in the same way as one regards the words of the prophets. Its purpose is to confirm what we see so that we can be more assured of God's will. It is a protection rather than a replacement of an individual's pursuit of God's will.

We should note one other point: This way of seeking God's will should be applied only to important matters. As to the trivial affairs of daily life, we do not need to resort to such a method. We can make judgments according to our common sense. Our God has not eradicated our common sense. God wants us to make our own judgments concerning things that we can manage with our common sense. We need to employ this method only in seeking God's will concerning the more important matters of our life.

In seeking God's will, we must not fall into an abnormal state where the mind is blank and the will is passive. Hebrews 5:14 speaks of those "who because of practice have their faculties exercised for discriminating between both good and evil." We need to exercise our mind and will. We have to put our will on God's side and co-labor with God. It is true that we should put aside our own will. But it is wrong to annul the function of the mind and the will, allowing them to be passive and void of function. Many people trust only in their intellect and not in God. This is a big mistake. But many people think that relying on God means that one does not need to use his mind. This is also a big mistake. When Luke wrote his gospel, it was "carefully investigated" (1:3). In Romans 12:2 Paul told us to "be transformed by the renewing of the mind that you may prove what the will of God is." In seeking God's will, we need to use our mind and our will. Of course, this mind and will have to be transformed and renewed by the Holy Spirit.

We need to briefly touch on the matter of visions and dreams as well. In the Old Testament God revealed His will to man through visions and dreams. In the New Testament there are also visions and dreams, but God does not use them as an essential means of guidance. In the New Testament the Spirit of God dwells in us and speaks to us directly from within. The chief and common means of guidance are the inward leading. God will lead us by dreams and visions only when He has something very important to say and it would not be easy for us to accept this leading under normal circumstances. In the New Testament visions and dreams are not the usual means of God's leading. Therefore, even when we have visions and dreams, we should still safeguard ourselves by seeking the inward confirmation and the confirmation in the environment. For example, Acts 10 shows us that God wanted Peter to preach the gospel to the Gentiles. Peter, being a Jew, would never go to the Gentiles according to his tradition. In order to turn him from this prejudice, God had to show him a vision. After Peter saw the vision, Cornelius sent three men to him. This was the confirmation in the environment. At the same time there was also the speaking of the Holy Spirit. These internal and environmental confirmations assured him that he was acting according to God's will.

Of course, there are cases when one has little time to consider or wait. At such times one can prove God's will immediately if the vision or dream is clear and obvious and the feeling within approves it; there is no need to wait for the confirmation in the environment. For example, Paul was in a trance when he was praying in the temple. He saw the Lord speaking to him and charging him to leave Jerusalem without delay. At first he reasoned with the Lord and tried to refuse. But the Lord said to him again, "Go, for I will send you forth far away to the Gentiles" (Acts 22:17-21). Later, Paul met a heavy storm at sea, and all hope of salvation was gone. God sent His angel to stand beside him and speak to him, telling him not to fear (27:23-24). These were all clear visions. But they do not occur frequently in the New Testament. God revealed things to His children in visions and dreams only when there was a special need. Some Christians have so many so-called dreams and visions that these are like every-day meals to them. This is a kind of spiritual sickness. It may come from some kind of nervous disorder, attack from Satan, or deception from evil spirits. Whatever the cause, this situation is abnormal.

In conclusion, God leads men by many ways. Everyone is different in his spiritual condition and needs. This is why God leads us in different ways. However, His main means are the arrangement in the environment, the inward leading, and the teachings in the Bible. We need to point out once again that when these three things are in line with one another, we can have the confidence that we have God's will.

IV. THOSE WHO ARE QUALIFIED TO KNOW GOD'S WILL

Finally, even if we have all the right methods, not everyone knows God's will. A right method is useful only when the person is also right. When the person is not right, even the right methods become useless. It is futile for a rebellious man to seek to know God's will. If a man wants to know God's will, he must have an inward yearning to do His will.

Deuteronomy 15:17 records the case of a slave who had his ear run through with an awl into the door. This shows that our ears have to listen to God's word all the time if we are to serve Him. We should come to the Lord and say, "I am willing to thrust my ear to the door. I will incline my ears to Your word. I want to serve You and do Your will. I beseech You from my heart. I will serve You. You are my Master. I have an earnest yearning within my heart to be Your slave. Let me hear Your word. Let me know Your will." We need to come before the Lord and plead for His word. We have to incline our ears and thrust them to the door. We have to wait for His commission and listen to His command.

Many times my heart aches over the fact that many people are looking for methods to know God's will, but they have no desire to obey God's will. They merely study such methods for the sake of knowledge. They have their own desires. They merely take God as their counselor and His will as their reference point. Brothers and sisters, God's will is made known only to those who are determined to obey His will! "If anyone resolves to do His will, he will know" (John 7:17). In order to know God's will, one must resolve to do His will. If you have an intense and absolute desire to do God's will, God will make known His will to you even when you know nothing about the methods. There is a word in the Bible: "For the eyes of the Lord run to and fro throughout the whole earth, to show Himself strong in the behalf of them whose heart is perfect toward Him" (2 Chron. 16:9). The literal translation of this verse is, "For the eyes of the Lord run to and fro throughout the whole earth, to show Himself strong on behalf of those whose heart is completely inclined towards Him." His eyes are running to and fro, from here to there. His eyes do not run through just once. Rather, they run continually to and fro to see whether anyone's heart is after His will. He will appear to those whose heart is completely inclined toward Him. If your heart is completely inclined toward the Lord and you say, "Lord, I want Your will; I really want it," God will show you His will. He will not refrain from revealing Himself to you; He has to reveal

Himself to you. We should not think that only those who have believed in the Lord for a long time can understand His will. We hope that every believer will offer up everything he has from the day that he is saved. This will pave the way for him to understand God's will.

We should never think that it is a trivial thing to know God's will. We are little worms in God's eyes. It is a tremendous thing for a tiny person like us to understand God's will! May we see that it is a glorious thing to understand God's will. Since God has humbled Himself to make His will known to man, we must seek to know His will, and we must worship, treasure, and do His will.